Red Flannel Petticoat

Muslin Drawers

Ready-made Corset

Embroidered White
Muslin Petticoat

Muslin Chemise

Chintz Robe and Muslin Nightgown

Silk Apron

January 1843—It's all official now. The announcements of our engagement are out. Matthew and I will be married in December next year. There is so much to do! Hardly know where to start for my trousseau and wedding things.

March 1843—Yesterday when the drummer came by, we traded eggs and a chicken for 20 yards of muslin and bought red calico at the exorbitant price of 75¢ a yard—enough for a new dress.

April 1843—We are cutting out my "unmentionables." Never had used a sewing bird before, but the one Matthew's mother sent me for Christmas is dandy. The tail is a spring clip that opens the beak to hold the goods for sewing long seams and tucks.

October 1843—Now all the white things are ready for embroidery. Matthew will doubtless be pleased with the pretty chintz robe made out of goods Mama was hoardin

November 1843—The aprons are all finished—2 of heavy "duck" and 1 of silk with ribbon bands. All ladies have black sil aprons for special.

Silk Bonnet

"Muslin de laine" Day Dress

Apron of Heavy "Duck"

Good Calico Dress with Brooch

Watermelon Pink Silk "Good" Dress

Stitched White Bonnet

December 1843—Christmas will be lonely without Matthew. But by this time next year he will be back from Texas Rangers' duty, and we will be married.

March 1944—Am working on a rather nice little dress out of the red calico, also one of "muslin de laine." It's a soft light-weight wool. Made it plain with just buttons down the front. One of my favorite things is the hand-me-down watermelon pink silk Mama's sister sent her from Tennessee and Mama altered to fit me. She said *she* wouldn't be going to anything fancy here on the frontier! For me, I think it's just right to wear to parties and visiting.

April 15, 1844—Matthew managed to get back to take me to a big dance at the Venables' last week. Wore my watermelon pink silk. It's odd to see such a variety of dress—homespun, calico, buckskin, and silk—side by side as we all danced on the hard-packed ground outside the cabin.

Black Felt Hat

Wool Frock Coat, Embroidered Satin Waistcoat,
Tucked Linen Shirt with Cravat

Kerseymere (Wool) Trousers

Matthew in Underdrawers and Everyday Shirt

Carpet Bag

For our wedding Matthew saved enough money to order a new black alpaca frock coat from Spencer, Lee & Walton—Men's Clothiers—in New Orleans. It cost him $36. He has neat, tight-fitting gray trousers with straps under the heels. His shirt is fine white linen made by his mother.

And best of all is his beautiful embroidered blue satin waistcoat that his uncle sent from Philadelphia. My, he will look handsome.

Oh yes, he has a new fancy—a white satin cravat that his uncle said is the latest fad in the east, instead of a neckcloth. His black felt hat, called a "gentleman's style," is one he ordered from New Orleans too. He said his carpet bag is all packed and ready for our trip to the "infare."

My dear Matthew is such a gentlemanly man!

Mantel Decorated for
Wedding Ceremony

Matrimonial Pincushion

Netted Mitts

Silk Reticule

Lace-trimmed
Handkerchief

Amanda in Chemise and Corset

Amanda's Silk Wedding Dress

We made my wedding dress using the silk goods ordered from New Orleans and going by a picture from *Godey's Lady's Book* that Samantha's mother gets from New York. We had blonde silk lace to edge the bertha. Mama embroidered my wedding pincushion and lined it with pale blue from my chintz robe, and she surprised me with my first ready-made corset and waxed orange blossoms for my coronet and bouquet. We have added fresh holly berries to liven up the bouquet.

December 24, 1844—Everything is ready. For something old, I have Grandmama's lace-trimmed handkerchief. For something new—my dress. Something borrowed—the mitts that Samantha lent me, and something blue is the ribbon on my chemise. Papa gave me a penny to wear in my shoe for good luck.

December 25, 1844—This is my wedding day. I feel an unspeakable joy! The sun is shining—a good omen for a happy day and a happy marriage. The circuit preacher is here from San Antonio and the ceremony will be in front of the fireplace where Mama arranged holly and evergreen with bows and candles. Matthew's family and folks from as far away as 30 miles will be here. Mama has been cooking for days—getting the wedding feast ready.

December 26, 1844—Today I write my new name for the first time—*Mrs. Matthew William Ritter*—I have become his partner for life. But I will always remain Amanda at heart.

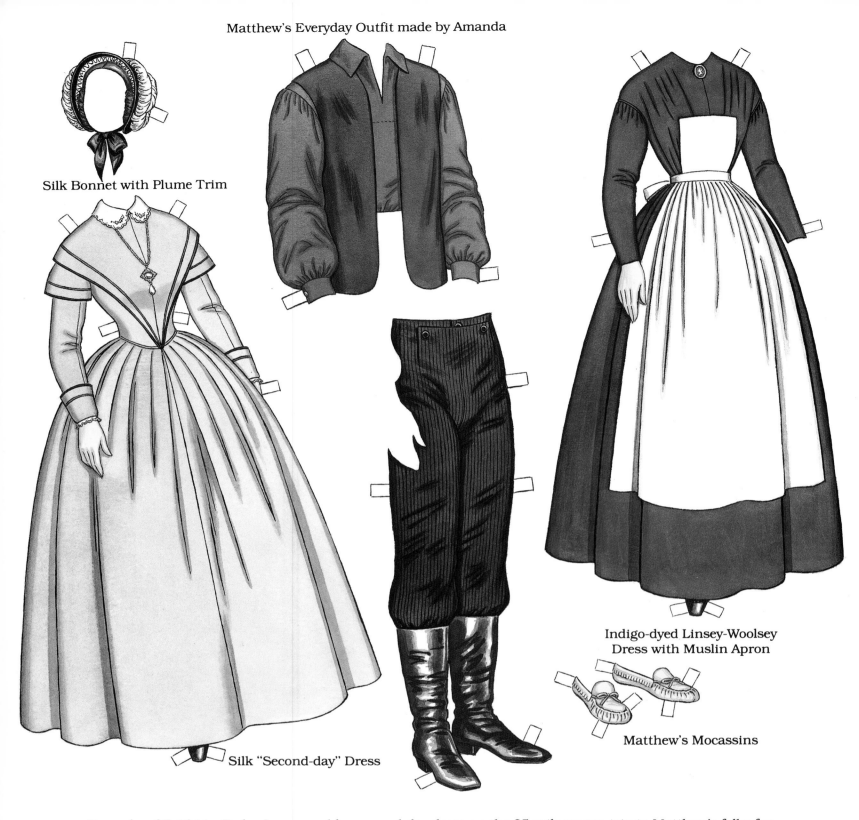

Matthew's Everyday Outfit made by Amanda

Silk Bonnet with Plume Trim

Silk "Second-day" Dress

Indigo-dyed Linsey-Woolsey
Dress with Muslin Apron

Matthew's Mocassins

December 27, 1844—Today I wore my blue second-day dress on the 25-mile wagon trip to Matthew's folks for the "infare" dinner. It was a scrumptious meal, and everyone said I was really looking fine in my silk dress with its piping in 2 shades of blue. It is the one Grandmama had made up by a dressmaker in Nashville, Tennessee, and mailed to me.

January 29, 1845—Matthew had staked a claim for land a few miles north of the falls on the Llano River about 45 miles from Austin. Just got settled in our own little 2-room cabin with limestone chimneys at each end and a loft room. Must start weaving again as I will be needing new things. But first Matthew needs some trousers and another vest for everyday.

June 1845—Bluebonnets are gone for the season, but I picked a bouquet of other beautiful bright wild flowers—firewheel, indian paintbrush, bluebells, and goldenrod. Also dried some wild strawberries to have in the winter months.

August 1845—I've learned to spin the wool very fine and have enough for a nice warm dress for everyday wear. Will dye the goods blue with indigo that grows wild around the hills.

September 1845—Traded an apron today for a pair of mocassins from a friendly Indian that comes around. Last week he took a loaf of bread for mocassins to fit Matthew.

November 1845—Made a long, bibbed white apron to wear when I hold the baby.

Embroidered Muslin Day Cap

Pin-stuck Maternity Cushion

WELCOME SWEET BABE

Amanda's Calico Nursing Dress

Bouquet of Wild Flowers

Amanda's Ombre Striped Cambric-Muslin Morning Dress
John Nathan in Christening Dress

December 1, 1845—The white linen christening dress is almost finished. Also the pin-stuck maternity cushion. It took so many pins to make the design—but Mama told me it was a social necessity for every new mother to have one. Besides, the pins will be useful.

December 29, 1845—Texas is now a state—the 28th. It is a good feeling to be a part of the United States and a relief to have the protection of the U.S. troops. I do love our lone star flag. It is the only flag with previous service as the flag of an independent nation.

January 10, 1846—Just took the last stitches on my printed calico nursing dress. An officer's wife I met at the frontier post—McCulloch's Station—let me borrow her dress to take the pattern. It was complicated and took me weeks to make. I try to keep the stitches small as it must be sturdy.

January 15, 1846—Now I can wear the little white cap that goes with the endearing term of "mother." Our beautiful little boy was born last week.

February 1846—Mama sent me a package with a new dress she had made in pretty shades of apricot. I will love wearing it. It's an apricot ombre cambric-muslin.

March 1846—The circuit preacher christened our baby, John Nathan, when he came through for service last Sunday. Wore my new apricot.

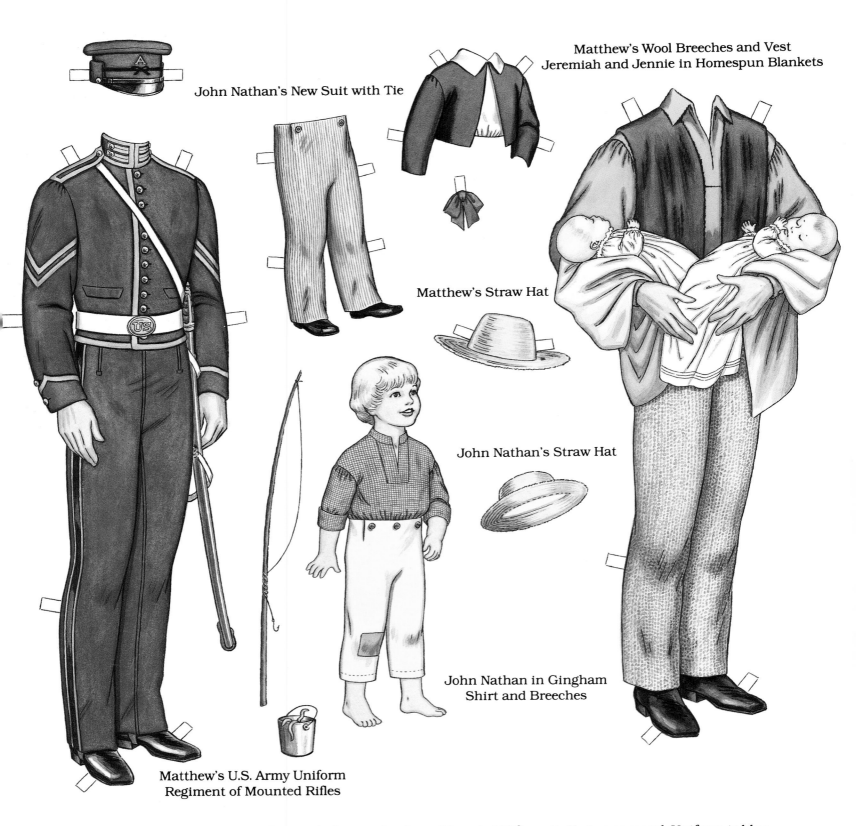

John Nathan's New Suit with Tie

Matthew's Wool Breeches and Vest
Jeremiah and Jennie in Homespun Blankets

Matthew's Straw Hat

John Nathan's Straw Hat

John Nathan in Gingham
Shirt and Breeches

Matthew's U.S. Army Uniform
Regiment of Mounted Rifles

June 1846—Matthew joined up with the regular Army Mounted Rifle unit. He is a corporal. Uniform is blue with gold braid and brass buttons. Black stripes piped with gold down the sides of the trouser legs. The corporal's stripes and waist belt and shoulder belt are white. He has a percussion rifle and a saber. He is in Company D. His "wheel hat" (cap) is blue with a black strap and visor.

June 15, 1846—The war is on with Mexico. Matthew left Monday. It's scarey without him. But I have my heart and mind properly regulated about his going. Indians raided the Dorsey place last week.

August 1846—Been drying fruit and filling the root cellar to get ready for winter. Collected honeybee wax and molded 5 dozen tapers. Gathered a nice basket of pecans from trees around the river.

November 1847—Finished heavy pants for Matthew out of the wool material he had bought at the post, also a gold chambray shirt and a brown wool vest. Want to have something new for him when he gets back.

June 1848—I rejoice to say Matthew is home! The war is over. And there is much work to do. I really need Matthew. Several of the neighbors offered to help with some log rollin' so we can add a room.

September 1850—Our family circle has been enlivened! Imagine . . . two babies at once. Our twins, Jeremiah and Jennie, were born last week. Matthew was at the fort when the babies came, but the Indian's squaw helped deliver them. Matthew came in right after and is proud as punch.

Rocking Horse for Jeremiah

Jennie and Jeremiah in Underclothes

Jennie's Doll

McGuffey's
First Eclectic Reader
for John Nathan

Jennie's Polka Dot Dress

Jeremiah's Chambray Dress

John Nathan's Wagon

Amanda's Reseda Green Cambric
Dress with Bonnet

Since he is four years old, John Nathan thinks he is big and important rocking the cradle and helping with the babies. Thank goodness, I managed to stitch him up a new suit a few weeks ago—a little dark jacket and striped duck pants. He wears his clothes so hard and is growing like a weed.

April 1852—Matthew says we'll go to Camp Meeting this summer. It pleasures me to think about it, but we'll need new clothes. Have some light reseda green cambric for a new dress. I'll trim it with ruffles and little embroidered borders if I have time. At least it will look cool! Think I'll make a nice bonnet to match.

May 1852—New dresses for the twins took a lot of time, with all the tucks. Matthew says he'll be glad when Jeremiah is old enough to wear trousers! John Nathan will have to wear the suit I made him before the twins came—even if the trousers are rather tight and short.

July 1852—Had a good time at Camp Meeting wearing my new green. It is hard with 2 babies to have time to visit much, but I did enjoy the singing. Matthew pitched a tent like everyone else. It made a little city of tents and we stayed for a whole week.

December 1854—Trying to get things ready for Christmas. I made Jennie a doll with black hair. Matthew made a rocking horse for Jeremiah and a sturdy little wagon for John Nathan. We also got him a *McGuffey's Reader*.

Bonnet with New Trim

Flowered Headdress

Ready-made Velvet-trimmed Cloak

Linen Walking Boots

"Made-over" Blue Silk Second-day Dress

Silk Ball Gown with Gauze Bertha

January 1858—I really need a ball gown. . . . Matthew's sister, Rebekah, is getting married in Austin in the fall. A real church wedding, with festivities. So exciting to think of going to the city. Will try reworking the cherry red tissue silk dress that was new when I got engaged. Mama gave me a flounce of lace-bordered gauze that will do a lovely bertha on a new, low neckline, and with some altering of the skirt panels I can get the wider look of the full bell skirt.

February 1858—Matthew went to Burnet today. The freighter had just delivered a shipment to the mercantile from New Orleans and Matthew picked a handsome tartan plaid taffeta that I will combine with the blue bengaline dress from my trousseau. By adding some flounces the skirt will look fuller—and I do have a new crinoline that will make it stand out nicely. Instead of 14 yards of goods, I'll be able to have a pretty up-to-date look with just 7 yards of the plaid and some new tassels.

March 1858—The wool cloak I ordered from Marshall Field in Chicago makes me feel so extravagant, but Matthew says I need something new after 14 years of marriage. I also ordered a pair of dancing slippers and little linen walking boots.

June 1858—Just like Christmas to have a package to open. One came on the stagecoach to the fort yesterday. It was my new cloak and is a beautiful dove gray wool with velvet trim. I had some striped taffeta ribbon, pink flowers and cherries saved back and am altering my old bonnet, again.

Puffed Muslin Chemisette

Velvet Bolero with Plain Chemisette

Striped Gingham Sunbonnet

Wool Merino Skirt

Amanda's Outdoor Working Garb

July 1858—Was able to find a length of black merino and a remnant of red velvet at the mercantile and will make a skirt and bolero. Then with 2 chemisettes it will be like having 2 dresses.

September 1858—We arrived in Austin today and it only took us two days to come the 45 miles in the wagon. Imagine real streets and even street lamps. There is a beautiful capitol building and more than 3,000 folks live here.

The wedding is tomorrow and I'll wear my blue bengaline, but I'll change into the red tissue silk for the ball. Makes me feel like Cinderella—especially since Mrs. Dorsey offered to keep the children for us.

October 1858—The wedding trip was wonderful—even though tiring. But now it is back to work and the endless routine.

March 1861—The states are all in a civil war. Matthew has had to go to the Army again. He will be a lieutenant in the 5th Texas Infantry. I will be so lonesome and busy. But the boys will do most of the work in the lots and fields, and Jennie helps me around the house. I'm having to do men's work again, like I did when Matthew was off in the Mexican War. No time to worry about what I wear.

January 31, 1862—We had everything ready for Christmas, in case Matthew came home, but the fighting was too critical. He wrote that he was injured in the Battle of Fredericksburg and wouldn't be able to travel. We must keep the home fires burning. I look forward with some impatience to the end of all this fighting.